Traditional GOJU-RYU KARATE

by Don Warrener

Traditional GOJU-RYU KARATE

by Don Warrener

......*in memory of*
Bob Dalgleish.....

Graphic Design Annette Hellingrath

ISBN   0-920129-02-1

1st   Printing 1982
2nd Printing 1985
3rd   Printing 1992

 MASTERS PUBLICATION

PRINTED IN HONG KONG

Dedication

This text is respectfully dedicated to Harold Warden, who with his 'Master Key' changed my life. I am deeply indebted to Harold forever.

Acknowledgement

I would like to acknowledge the diligent work of our photographer Mr. Paul Hourigan. Also, my right arm Annette Hellingrath whose layouts and artistic touches cannot be replaced. Phil McColl, Trevor Peroune and Terry O'Donnell for assisting me in the photos.

A special thank you to my teacher Sensei Richard Kim for giving me additional background information on the Goju Ryu katas used in this book.

CONTENTS:

INTRODUCTION

Preface

Of all the books published, this is the first one I know of done on Goju Ryu Katas.

The purpose of this book is to fill a void in the Martial Artists' library and as well to act as a training manual for those who want to learn the katas of Goju Ryu. Also, the basic techniques of this old but illustrious style of unarmed combat.

'Traditional Goju Ryu Karate' has been in the making for the last five years and is now ready for students of the Martial Arts.

The Goju style is one that employs low stances with fast circular arm techniques. Its Chinese origins can be seen in the katas if you look closely.

It is important to note that although some of the moves to the katas may be different from the style of Goju Ryu that you are practicing, this should not be of great concern since there are many styles of Goju Ryu, Japanese, Okinawan, U.S.A., Canadian Goju Ryu to name a few.

The important facet to remember is that the schematics of the kata are the same.

History of Goju-Ryu

Miyagi, born Miyagusuku (later changed to Miyagi Chojun by the Japanese) in Naha Okinawa on April 25, 1888, to a noble family, started his life in Karate at the age of nine. His first teacher was Higashionna sensei. By the time Miyagi was 20 years old, he was his sensei's disciple.

Miyagi Chojun later travelled to central China where he studied Zen as well as the Martial Arts as his sensei before him had done. (Many styles of kung fu were adapted to the originators' environment. North of China, for example, being very hilly would develop the lower body making it stronger for kicking. Whereas Southern China, covered with bodies of water, developed the upper body through rowing and such).

After many years, Miyagi returned to Okinawa and formulated the Goju Ryu system of karate, utilizing the principles his sensei taught him. After the system of Goju Ryu had taken shape, he felt the need for a symbolic insignia. He simply copied his clenched fist (slightly crooked because of a previous injury). Blending the strong snap techniques of the Okinawan style and the dynamic and free techniques of the soft Chinese Kenpo, his style was complete.

It was while attending Retsumeikan University that Yamaguchi Sensei, a deeply religious man, first heard of Goju Karate and of the great Okinawan Miyagi Chogun.   Curious about the system, Yamaguchi sensei (sometimes called 'The Cat') wrote to Miyagi and invited him to come to Japan.   Miyagi accepted and left shortly thereafter.

The meeting of the two was to be a fateful one, not only for Goju but for all karate.

Yamaguchi sensei immediately fell in love with the strange and intricate patterns displayed by Miyagi.   The hard and soft approach was for him.

The word Goju means hard and soft. 'Go' is the Japanese word for hardness and 'ju' is the word for softness. The system is based on an Oriental concept that all hardness and stiffness is not good. At the same time all softness and too much gentleness is not good. The two should complement each other. Combining the two gives Goju Ryu karate its beautiful, disciplined movements, filled with grace, flowing forms and strength. Actions are sometimes extremely fast and other times slow and majestic. Goju Ryu relies on an aggressive style of attack with emphasis on delivering blows 'hard' but with easy effort and rapid succession, maneuvering not only forwards and backwards. As well as from side to side and aiming from outside in and inside straight on.

When Miyaji Chojun sensei left Japan to return to Okinawa he left behind him a well-trained and dedicated follower in Goju Ryu.

The first thing Yamaguchi did was set about establishing a dojo. He organized the first dojo in Western Japan in 1930.   Under his capable leadership the school attracted new adherents and the Goju Ryu karate began to fan out across the island nation.

Early in the Japanese development, Yamaguchi sensei made fundamental changes in the Goju school that were to radically alter the course of karate.   After observing his students he came to the conclusion that the strict Okinawan brand of karate, with its Chinese origins was too static and limited in style. He believed that just the practice steps in sparring called kumite inhibited many students, so he devised free style kumite or sparring at first along the lines of boxing. After that it was a natural step of progression to go to free style sparring.   Later, the sparring or kumite underwent further transformation using knowledge of the other martial arts to improve it still more.

By freeing karate from the strict adherence to kata and the adaptations of the competitive element, Goju made tremendous advances in the next few years.

In 1930, Masters succeded in their efforts to have karate admitted into the Butoku Kai, the official government headquarters

for the Japanese martial arts. That same year Goju headquarters were established in Tokyo next to the famous Giho Kai Judo Institute.

From here the Second World War came and ended, leaving servicemen from all parts of the world training and taking the art back home, spreading Goju through a vast network of dojos, in schools, offices, factories, etc.

In 1953, Miyagi sensei passed away, leaving Meitoku Yagi to succeed him in Okinawa and with Yamaguchi sensei continuing his efforts in expanding the art in Japan. The decision to relocate the headquarters of all Japan karate, Goju Kai organizations in Tokyo in 1950 resulted in a great jump for population for the Goju system.

Besides Japan, Goju organizations exist in Thailand, Hong Kong, Korea, Formosa, the Philippines, Australia, West Germany, Italy, Great Britain, Mexico, Canada and the United States.

Tenets of Goju Ryu Karate Do

"We who are studying karate do aspire to these virtues."

1. We are proud to study the spirit of Goju.

2. We shall practice courtesy.

3. We shall be quick to seize opportunity.

4. We shall always practice patience.

5. We shall always keep the fighting spirit of karate.

This poem is one I base my life on.

A New Day.....

This is the beginning of a new day.

God has given me this day to use as I will.

I can waste it or use it for good,

but what I do today is important because

I am exchanging a day of my life for it!

When tomorrow comes this day will be gone forever,

leaving in its place something that I have traded for it.

I want it to be gain, and not loss,

good and not evil; success and not failure;

in order that I shall not regret

the price that I have paid for it.

1.) Author in Japan with Master Gogen Yamaguichi ('The Cat').

Photos of the past

3.) 1968 author in first dojo.

2.) 1968 with Kung Fu Master Frank Lee.

4.) Author pictured with Professor Wally Jay & Richard Kim.

6.) 1981 Middle East tour.

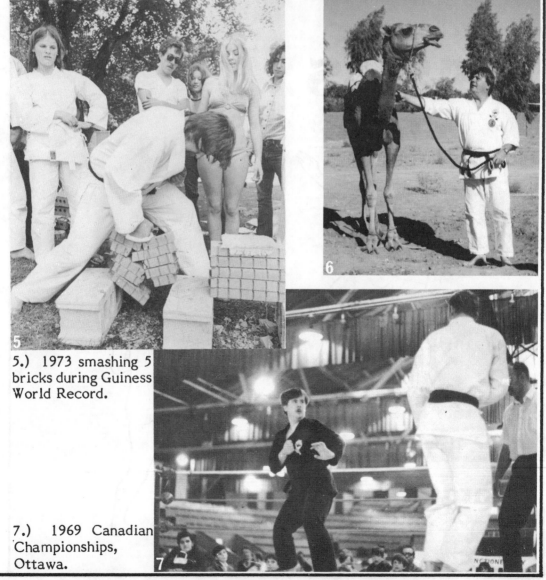

5.) 1973 smashing 5 bricks during Guiness World Record.

7.) 1969 Canadian Championships, Ottawa.

BASICS

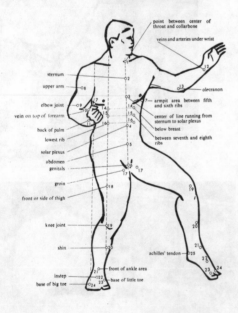

point between center of throat and collarbone
veins and arteries under wrist
sternum
upper arm
olecranon
elbow joint
armpit area between fifth and sixth ribs
vein on top of forearm
center of line running from sternum to solar plexus
back of palm
below breast
lowest rib
between seventh and eighth ribs
solar plexus
abdomen
genitals
groin
front or side of thigh
knee joint
shin
achilles' tendon
front of ankle area
instep
base of big toe
base of little toe

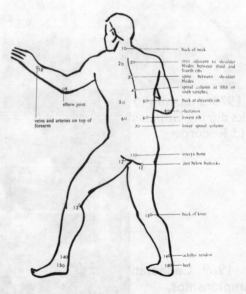

back of neck
area adjacent to shoulder blades between third and fourth ribs
spine between shoulder blades
spinal column at fifth or sixth vertebra
back at eleventh rib
elbow joint
olecranon
lower rib
lower spinal column
veins and arteries on top of forearm
coccyx bone
just below buttocks
back of knee
achilles tendon
heel

Target points

16

Points on Basics

STANCES

(1) Power is rooted in the feet, developed by the knees and directed by the hips.
(2) Without a strong foundation (stance), strikes and blocks will be minimal in effect.

HAND TECHNIQUES

(1) The principals of expansion and contraction are a must when striking and as well for blocking.
(2) Kime is the focusing of one's energy at the moment contact is made and the technique is fully executed. This energy focusing must be done by locking each and every muscle of your body as you strike.
(3) The angle of the attack is extremely important to maximize the effect of the strike.

KICKING TECHNIQUES

(1) Remember to curl your toes for each and every kick (excluding instep roundhouse kick).
(2) You must remember to use proper joint sequence. All kicks follow the same pattern, start with the hips, work to the knee and finish with the ankle.
(3) Remember to keep your base foot flat on the ground, otherwise you will lose your balance.

BLOCKING TECHNIQUES

(1) 90% of blocks are executed with the front hand, making it easier to counter.
(2) In Goju Ryu, we try to block every attack with two blocking techniques to make sure the attacker does not get through.

GENERAL POINTS

(1) The most important quality of basics is the technique. A properly executed technique breeds both power and speed.
(2) Remember that all karate techniques start in what is known as 'the box' (the abdomen area).
(3) Any fighting blow should be supplemented or enhanced with a kiai, which is a short one syllable word. A kiai is forced out by tightening the entire body. Example of kiai you can use Di! Ki! Das! Yi!

17

Terminology

Dachi-*Stance*

Sanchin Dachi - Power stance
Zenkutsu Dachi - Forward stance
Sheko Dachi - Straddle stance
Heiko Dachi - Natural stance
Musubu Dachi - Ready stance
Neko Ashi Dachi - Cat stance

Geri-Kick

Mae Geri - Front kick
Kensetsu Geri - Joint kick
Yoko Geri - Side kick
Fumi Komi Geri - Stomp kick

Uke-Blocks

Hariatoshi - 3 point low block
Kake Uke - Hooking block
Mawashi Uke - Roundhouse block
Age Uke - High block
Uchi Uke - Inside block
Soto Uke - Outside block
Gedan Barai - Low sweeping block
Kakuto Uke - Chicken head block
Teisho Uke - Palm block

Te-Hand Strikes

Oizuke - Lunge punch
Gyaku Zuke - Reverse punch
Kizama Zuke - Jab punch
Shuto - Knifehand
Teisho - Palm heel
Empi - Elbow
Rekkan - Backfist
Nukite - Finger strike
Mawashi Zuke - Hook punch

General Terms

Sensei - teacher
Dojo - training hall
Gi - uniform
Kia - yell
Kimi - focus
Kyu - boy
Dan - man
Yemai - stop
Ashimai - begin
Obi - belt
Rei - bow
Kilskai - attention
Kumite - sparring
Kata - forms
Kihon - basics
O'Sensei - teacher's teacher
Mukso - meditate
Nippon - Japan

Stances

Heiko Dachi - natural stance
(1) Feet are pointing straight ahead and are shoulder width apart.

Sanchin Dachi - power stance
(2) The most basic and powerful of all Goju stances. This stance is simply referred to as the hourglass stance. Feet are shoulder width apart with the front foot turned inwards and the back foot's heel turned slightly outwards. Knees are pushed together and bent. Hips are contracted in an upwards position.

Zenkutsu Dachi - forward stance
(3) Again feet are shoulder width apart and approximately 2½ shoulder width in length. The front knee is bent out over the big toe and pushed to the outside. The back leg is locked straight.

Sheko Dachi - straddle stance
(4) The Sheko Dachi stance is the same length as the Zenkutsu Dachi stance, the only difference being the fact that both knees are bent equally out over the toes which are pointed outwards.

Neko Ashi Dachi - cat foot stance
(5) The back leg supports 90% of the weight, while the front foot (raised high on the ball of the foot), is used only for balancing. Length is approximately one shoulder width, back leg at a 45° angle, front straight ahead.

Hand Techniques

Gyaku Zuki - reverse punch
(1) Right side is forward in on guard position. (2) Left hand has returned to Chamber ready for the attack. (3) Left hand strikes attacker's solar plexus.

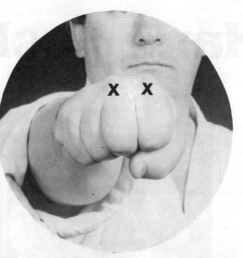

Kizama Zuki - jab punch
(1) Left hand is in on guard position ready for attack. (2) Without stepping forward left hand begins the punch to the face. (3) Left hand continues aiming for attacker's jaw. (Take note that the left foot is forward and without taking a step forward the left hand executes the attack).

Hand Techniques

Shuto - knife hand
(1) Left hand is in a cocked ready position, ready to strike. (2) The hand strikes out aiming for the neck area, hitting with the meaty inside part of the hand.

Oi Zuki - lunge punch
(1) The attacker on right is in on guard position.   (2) He begins to explode forward while driving his left hand to chamber. (3) He continues to drive in, thrusting with his left foot forward, left hand to the face.

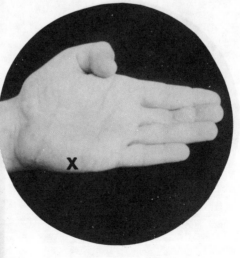

25

Hand Techniques

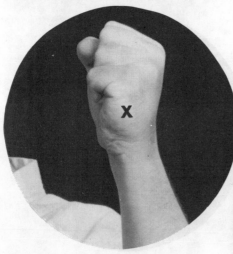

Tettsui - the bottom fist strike
(1) Right hand is raised above the head ready to strike. (2) Drive elbow down, moving fist ready to smash attacker's head. (3) The far arm snaps down, driving into attacker, hitting with the bottom of the fist.

Hand Techniques

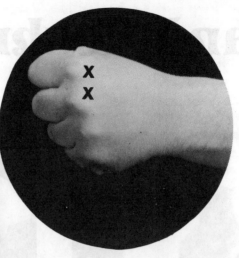

Rekkan - back hand
(1) Defender on right readies to counter by bringing his right hand to shoulder height. (2) He slides into horse stance beginning the backhand strike by moving the elbow towards the attacker. (3) He then snaps his fist outward, hitting with the back of the hand.

Hand Techniques

Haito - ridge hand
(1) Right hand is brought to the outside getting ready to arc in towards attacker's head. (2) The thumb is tucked in and the hand moves towards the target area, the temple. Strike with the ridge of the hand.

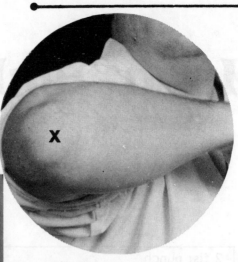

Empi - elbow strike
(There are many varieties of this strike, the one shown is one of the more common ones.)
(1) Defender on right has just completed the block. (2) He begins to get ready for the elbow strike by withdrawing right hand to left side. (3) He then very simply smashes his elbow into attacker's rib cage as shown. (For added power, make sure hand is clenched into a tight fist).

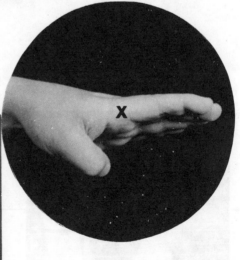

Hand Techniques

Ni Zuki - 2 fist punch
(This technique is uncommon but is used in several of the katas).
(1) Simply, it's a double fist punch to the head and stomach area, done simultaneously. (2) Take note, the stomach punch has the palm up and the head punch has the palm down.

Nukite - finger tips
(1) Ready for attack. (2) Only the weak areas of the body are attacked with this technique (eyes or throat).

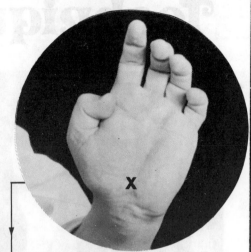

2

Teisho - palm heel strike
(One of the most powerful techniques the hands can deliver).
(1) Right hand readies to strike out.
(2) Using the head of the hand, connect with the jaw.

1

2

Kicking Techniques

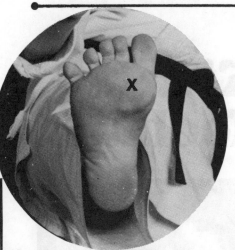

Mae Geri - front kick
(1) On guard position. (2) Right leg comes up into chamber. (3) As the foot moves out the hip is thrust in, giving maximum power to the technique.

Yoko Geri - side kick
(1) On guard position. (2) Right leg shifts up to the left. (3) Bring left leg up in chambered position, ready for completion of kick position. (4) Left foot strikes out hitting with the heel of the foot.

Kicking Techniques

Kicking
Techniques

Mawashi Geri - roundhouse kick
(1) On guard position. (2) Right leg is raised to the chambered position parallel to the floor. (3) The foot snaps out aiming for the head, hitting with either the instep or the ball of the foot.

Ushiro Geri - back kick
(1) On guard position. (2) Left leg steps across in front. (3) Turn to your right looking over your right shoulder ready to deliver right back kick. (4) Drive right foot into opponent's mid-section, hitting with the heel and the bottom of the foot.

Kicking Techniques

Hiza Geri - knee kick
(1) Left leg has begun to move. (2) The knee is raised up and begins to drive in. (3) Left knee smashes into abdomen area.

Fumi Komi - stomping kick
(1) Attacker has been dropped to the floor. (2) Right leg is raised in chamber position ready to stomp down. (3) Right foot stomps down, hitting attacker with heel.

Kicking Techniques

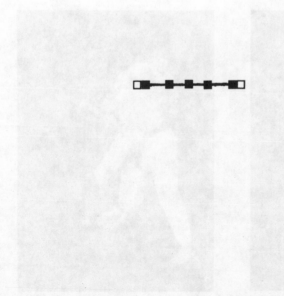

Mikasuki Geri - crescent kick
(1) On guard position. (2) Using right leg, swing up along the outside of the attacker, head height. (3) Continue the arcing motion and drive your leg into the side of his head.

Blocking Techniques

Gedan Barai - low block
(1) On guard position. (2) The left hand comes to the right ear, right hand is straight. (3) Left hand drives down blocking with forearm, using expansion.

Age Uke - rising block
(1) On guard position. (2) Attacker's right fist strikes toward defender's face as he begins to block up. (3) The left hand continues moving up blocking the attack successfully. (Turn palm up and be sure to use expansion of the upper torso).

41

Blocking Techniques

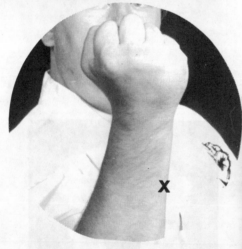

Soto Uke - outside middle area block
(1) On guard position. (2) Left arm is raised up high, ready to smash down on attacker's forearm. (3) Left arm drives down, blocking the attacker as the right hand is brought to chamber. (On this block use contraction of the stomach muscles).

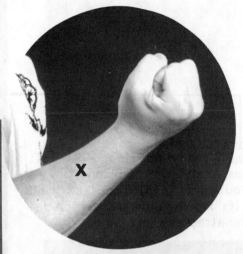

3

Uchi Uke - inside block
(1) On guard position.   (2) Left arm comes back underneath rib cage (right side) right arm extends out in front. (3) Using expansion block with the inside of your left arm clearing the way for an attack, should it be necessary.

2

3

Kake Uke - hooking block
(1) On guard ready position. (2) Left hand comes across the body and begins to block outwards. (3) The left hand continues its hooking outward motion deflecting the attacker's left hand.

1

2

4

2

3

3

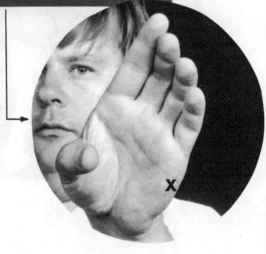

X

5

<u>Mawashi Uke</u> - roundhouse block
(1) On guard ready position. (2) Hands get into position for block, right hand on left elbow. (3) Right hand blocks high, while left hand blocks low. (4) Hands continue to move around in a circular pattern with the right hand low and the left hand high. (5) Both hands come in, left hand to the arm pit, right hand to right hip. Then both hands strike out, left to face, right to groin, using palm heels.

Blocking Techniques

Hariatoshi - 3 point lower block
(1) On guard ready position. (2) Shift into Sheko Dachi and raise left hand high, right hand across the body. (3) Left upper arm blocks the first strike. (4) Left hand continues its arcing movement downward, blocking the second strike. (5) Continues down to its final position blocking the third strike.

Blocking Techniques

Teisho Uke – palm heel block
(1) On guard position.   (2) As the attacker's right hand strikes, block using left palm heel as depicted in photo.

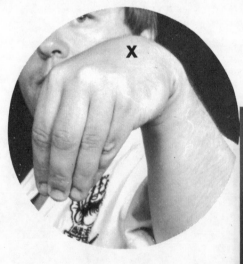

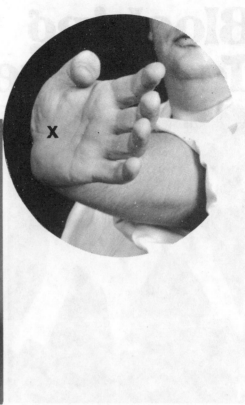

Kakuto Uke - chicken head block
(1) On guard position. (2) As attacker's right hand strikes, defender's left hand bends, blocking up and deflecting the attack.

Blocking Techniques

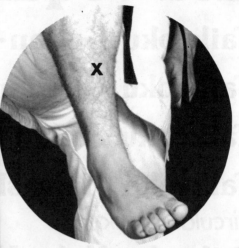

3

Hiza Uke - shin block
(1) On guard ready position. (2) Defender on left leans back on right leg raising left as attackers front kick homes in. (3) He continues the block by raising his left leg high.

kata requirements

Taikyoku Gedan-lst *course lower*

Taikyoku Chudan-lst *course middle*

Taikyoku Jodan-lst *course upper*

Taikyoku Mawashi Uke-lst *course circular block*

Taikyoku Kake Uke-lst *course hooking block*

Gekisai Itch-attack & smash 1

Gekisai Ni-attack & smash 2

Sanchin-3 battles

Tensho-turning

Saifa-destroy, defeat

Seienchin-attack, conquer, suppress

Sanseiru-36 movements

Shi Sho Chin-27 movements

Seisun-56 movements

Seipai-18 movements

1st Dan

2nd 3rd 4th

10 points on kata

1 All kata must begin and end on the same spot. This symbolizes the philosophy of life, that we all come into the world the same way and leave the same way.

2 Each kata must be announced strongly, with feeling, to establish a fighting spirit.

3 Perfect kata must be developed around these six points:

1. Eyes - look before you move to a new direction and do it with intensity.
2. Breathing - inhale and exhale in the proper places.
3. Kia - the kia or scream must be done with feeling.
4. Focus - the expansion and contraction must be used in the proper places.
5. Pace - like good music, good kata has a rhythm.
6. Technique - without proper technique it isn't a kata.

4 The first and last moves of a kata are the most important. This sets the trend for the rest of the kata and sets the attitude that you leave with.

5 When doing a kata your opponent is you. You make or break the form. You are in control, unlike a kumite match.

6 When doing kata you must visualize the attackers, imagining isn't enough - visualize.

7 Kata is the means by which a martial artist practices self-improvement.

8 Try to perfect one or two katas, three at the most. Remember quality is better than quantity.

9 Before doing each kata, take the opportunity during the mukso to talk to yourself convincing yourself this will be the best form you have ever done.

10 There are four steps to mastering the kata:

1. Learn the schematics of the kata.
2. Learn the rhythm of the kata.
3. Realize attackers and opponents while doing the kata.
4. Become one with the kata.

*Kiai point in katas

TAIKYOKU GEDAN

⟨first course lower area⟩

Interpreted as the First Course Lower. This preparatory form emphasizes the sheko dachi and develops the Hariatoshi block, which is a 3point lower block. It follows the basic H pattern which is the pattern used for all 5 of the Taikyoko katas.

Goju katas, Meaning and Tradition — by Richard Kim

The following delineation of Goju katas are meant to help those who want to delve into the historical and philosophical aspects of the katas. The "how" of the katas can be learned and gleaned from the photos and explanations that are specifically set up for that purpose. The explanations set forth, herewith, in general historical context ought to give an aspiring student as to the "why" and put him in the philosophical mold it was intended to do.

3

6

Gedan

Ready stance (1), left hand on right hand with feet spread at 45°, mucso posture (2). Left and right heels have moved out (3) hands are back to back. Inhale deeply. While exhaling (4) pull both hands to your side and position your feet in Heiko Dachi stance. Move right leg backwards (5) into a Shiko Dachi stance at a 45° angle (all stances in this kata are at a 45° angle), simultaneously doing a Hariotoshi block. Stepping straight forward (6) with your right foot doing a right lunge punch in Shiko Dachi. Having moved your right foot 180° behind you (7) to your right, simultaneously doing a Hariatoshi block. Step forward (8) with your left foot while executing a lunge punch. (9) Move your left foot and left hand to your left doing a Hariatoshi block again.

8

9

12*

Gedan

Step forward with your right foot (10) and do a right lunge punch. Step forward again (11) doing a left lunge punch. (12) Step forward once again executing a right lunge punch, KIAI at this point. Move your left foot around behind you 180° (13) and do a left low block. Step ahead (14) and do a right lunge punch. (15) Move your right foot around 180° to your right simultaneously doing a low right block. Step straight ahead (16) and do a left lunge punch. Move your left foot and your left hand 90° to your left (17) and block downwards with a Hariatoshi block. (18) Step straight ahead and do a right lunge punch.

14

17

18

20*

Gedan

Step straight in again (19) and do a left lunge punch. (20) Step in again doing a right lunge punch and KIAI. Move your left foot around behind you (21) 180° and do a left low block. Step in again (22) doing a right lunge punch. (23) Move your right foot and hand around to your right 90°, doing a low Hariatoshi block. After having brought your right foot back to the left, knees slightly bent, breathe in, (24) both hands come up in front, signifying the end of the kata. Both hands have been pulled to the chest (25) rotated so that palms are facing down. The adherent now presses down using proper Goju breathing (26). Return both hands to side (27) in the same position used when starting kata.

23

26

27

TAIKYOKU CHUDAN
⟨first course middle area⟩

Interpreted as the First Course Middle area. This form deals with the uchi uke block and also the lunge punch, done in zen kutsu dachi.

Chudan

Mucso position (1). On guard ready position (2). Move right foot 90° to right (3), doing left middle block in Sanchin stance. Step straight in (4) with the right foot doing right lunge punch. Moving 180° to your right doing middle block (5). Step straight in (6) doing lunge punch. (7) Move left foot 90° to your left doing left middle block. Step straight in with right lunge punch (8).

Chudan

Step in with left lunge punch (9). Step in with right lunge punch (10) KIAI point. Move left foot 90° behind you (11) with left foot, doing middle block. (12) Step straight in with right lunge punch. Move right foot 180° to your right (13) doing right middle block. (14) Step straight in with left lunge punch. Move left foot 90° to left (15), left middle block. (16) Step forward with right lunge punch.

18*

21

Chudan

(17) Step straight ahead left lunge punch. Step in with right lunge punch (18). KIAI point. (19) Move left foot 90° around behind you doing a left middle block. (20) Step straight in with right lunge punch. Move right foot 90° to your right (21), doing a right middle block. Move right foot back to a standing position (22) right hand on top of left. Turn hands over and down to finish kata (23).

23

TAIKYOKU JODAN
〈first course upper area〉

Interpreted as <u>First</u> <u>Course</u> <u>Upper</u>. This form teaches the high block jodan uke done in Sanchin Dachi. Also, the lunge punch done in zen kutsu dachi.

Jodan

(1) Mucso position, meditation posture. (2) On guard, ready to go position in Heiko Dachi stance. Move your right foot (3) and do a high left Jodan block, as you turn to your left, in Sanchin stance. (4) Lunge straight ahead in Zenkutsu Dachi stance doing a lunge punch with the right hand. Turn 180° (5) to your right moving the right foot into Sanchin stance, doing a high block. Step straight in doing a left lunge punch in forward stance (6). Move your left foot 90° to your left (7) into Sanchin stance doing a left high block. Step forward (8) doing a lunge punch, forward stance right side. Step forward doing a left lunge punch (9).

10

12

13

15

16

Jodan

Step forward into a right lunge punch and KIAI at this point (10). Turn 90° to your left (11) moving your left foot into Sanchin stance doing a high block. (12) Step forward executing a right lunge punch in forward stance. Turn 180° to your right (13) moving right foot into Sanchin stance doing a high block. Step straight in (14) doing a left lunge punch. Turn 90° to your left (15) in Sanchin stance doing left high block moving left foot. Step straight in (16) forward stance, right lunge punch. (17) Step in with left lunge punch forward stance. Step in right foot, right hand lunge punch (18) KIAI point.

19

23

22

Jodan

Move left foot behind you to your left (19), Sanchin stance, left high block. (20) Step in with the right foot, forward stance, right lunge punch. Move right foot 90° to your right in Sanchin stance (21) facing straight ahead, doing right front block. (22) Move right foot back to standing position right hand on top of left. Turn hands over and down (23) to finish kata.

TAIKYOKU MAWASHI UKE
⟨first course roundhouse block⟩

Interpreted as First Course Roundhouse Block. This kata teaches the Mawashi Uke or circular blocking of Goju Ryu. It also begins teaching blocking and counter attacking combinations.

Mawashi Uke

(1) Mucso position. (2) On guard ready position. Move your right foot out so that you are now facing to the left in a Sanchin stance, (3) hands are in the starting position of the Mawashi Uke. (4) Hands have started the Mawashi Uke block. Hands have completed the Mawashi Uke block (5). (6) Hands are pushed outwards, one to the jaw, one to the groin, completing the block. From this point the left hand juts out open (7) while the right hand is returned to chamber. Right foots comes up to left. (8) The right foot steps forward, right elbow smashes left palm.

Mawashi Uke

Right back fist is executed (9). Right hand drops down (10) to low Hariatoshi block. Left reverse punch, done in Zenkutsu Dachi stance (11).

9

The next moves in the Mawashi Uke follows the same pattern as Taikyoku Gedan. The difference is only technical, not directional. In Taikyoku Mawashi Uke, you do a Mawashi Uke block, the same as moves 3, 4, 5 and 6. Wherever you did a Hariatoshi block in Taikyoku Gedan. Then in Taikyoku Mawashi Uke you do the combination of elbow, backfist, block punch, wherever you did the single lunge punch in Taikyoku Gedan, follow the same pattern as Taikyoku Gedan.

10   11

TAIKYOKU KAKE-UKE
⟨first course hooking block⟩

Interpreted as <u>First Course Hooking Block</u>. The kake uke done in Sanchin. The hand combination again stresses the usage of hips in both blocking and counterattacking for maximum power.

Kake Uke

(1) Mucso position. (2) On guard ready position. Right foot has moved so that you face to the left (3) in left Sanchin stance. Right hand crosses left, ready for Kake Uke block. (4) Kake Uke block is completed. Right foot moves up to left, left hand extends outward for elbow strike (5). (6) Right foot continues forward in Shiko Dachi, right elbow strikes left open hand. Right hand flies out (7) in a backfist, while the left hand returns to chamber. (8) Right hand drops down to Hariatoshi block. Left hand shoots out doing Gyakiu Suki (9) while the left foot locks out into forward stance.

From here on in the Taikyoku Kake Uke follows the same pattern as Taikyoku Gedan. The difference is only technical, not directional. In Taikyoku Kake Uke, you do a Kake Uke block, the same as move 4, wherever you did a Hariatoshi block in Taikyoku Gedan. Then in Taikyoku Kake Uke you do the combination of elbow backfist, block punch. Wherever you did the single lunge punch in Taikyoku Gedan, follow the same pattern as Taikyoku Gedan.

GEKISAI-ITCH
⟨attack & smash⟩ ⟨1⟩

Interpreted as <u>Attack and Smash</u>. This kata is of recent vintage. In fact, it was designed by Miyagi Chojun after the war - World War Two. It was formerly practiced with the open hand. This kata introduces the three fundamental blocks - jodan -chudan - gedan. It also introduces the fundamental attacks and stances.

3

5

Gekisai Itch

(1) Mucso position. (2) On guard ready position. (3) Right foot moves outwards, left high block. Right lunge punch (4). Left heel moves in to form Shiko Dachi stance (5). Right foot comes straight back (6) readying for the turn. (7) Untwist, raising your left hand and readying for Hariatoshi block. Perform Hariatoshi block (8). (9) Move left foot to your right and do a right high block.

8

9

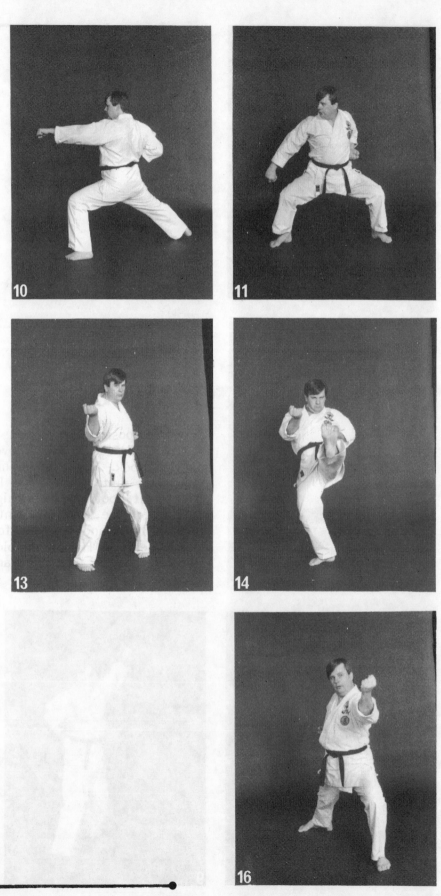

Gekisai Itch

(10) Step straight in with left lunge punch. Step backwards, doing right Hariatoshi block (11) repeating steps 5, 6, 7 and 8. (12) Move left foot forward in Sanchin doing left middle block. Step forward again, (13) doing right middle block. Stepping in, do a left front kick (14). Step down in Zenkutsu Dachi doing left elbow strike (15). (16) Do left backfist. Shift into Shiko Dachi (17) and do a Hariatoshi block with your left hand. (18) Do a right reverse punch.

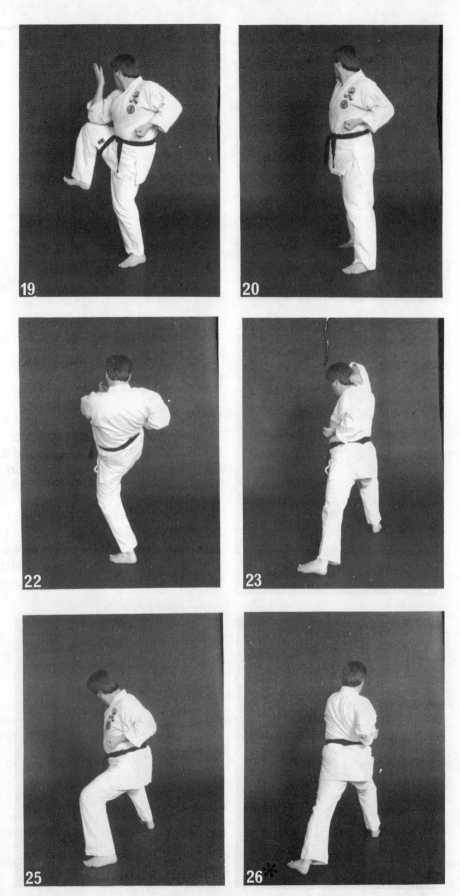

Gekisai Itch

Lift right leg up (19) and move right elbow, touch right knee, right hand open. Step down into Heiko Dachi (20) doing a right Shuto to the throat. (21) Step forward with left foot doing left middle block. (22) Step in again doing right front kick. (23) Step down, doing a right elbow to jaw. (24) Do a right back fist. (25) Shift back into Shiko Dachi doing a right Hariatoshi block. Follow this with a left reverse punch (26). Lift left knee up, (27) touch it to your left elbow. (28) Step down into natural stance, doing left Shuto to throat.

31

34

Gekisai Itch

Step back at 45° angle with the left foot in Zenkutsu Dachi stance, ready hands for a Mawashi Uke block and double punch (29). Hands are readied for double punch (30). Both hands strike out, (31) one on top of the other doing double punch. Bring left foot up to right foot, right hand is closed in a fist (32). Left hand is open and both knees are slightly bent. Bring both hands back to your sides quickly (33). Move your right foot back 45° (34) right hand is up readying for Mawashi Uke block and double punch. (35) Both hands are readied for punch. Both hands strike out (36) one on top of the other. Right foot moves up to the left (37) ending the form. Both hands have turned over and are back in place (38) end of kata.

37

38

GEKISAI-NI
⟨attack & smash⟩⟨2⟩

This kata is interpreted the same as the Gekisai Itch. Starts on the advanced stances and hand techniques but it primarily has the same fundamentals as Gekisai Itch

Gekisai Ni

(1) Mukso position. (2) On guard ready position. (3) Right leg has stepped out and the left hand has performed a high block. (4) Stepping forward in forward stance, perform right lunge punch. (5) Moving right back into Shiko Dachi stance, perform a left Hariatoshi block. Moving left leg, execute right high block (6). (7) Stepping in, do a left lunge punch. (8) Moving left leg back into Shiko Dachi, perform a right Hariatoshi block. (9) Moving left leg forward into Sanchin stance, execute a left Kake Uke block.

Gekisai Ni

(10) Stepping forward with the right leg, execute a right Kake Uke block. (11) Deliver a left front kick to the mid section. (12) Stepping down, execute a left elbow strike. (13) Then a left back knuckle. (14) Next do a Hariatoshi block. (15) Kiai while executing a powerful right reverse punch. (16) Raise the right knee to the right elbow readying for attack. (17) Step down into natural stance and deliver a right Shuto to the throat area. (18) Move the left leg forward into Sanchin stance and do a left Kake Uke block.

11

12

14

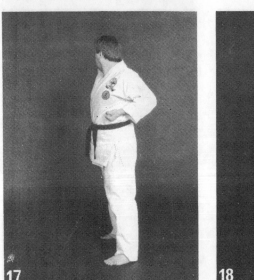

17

18

Gekisai Ni

Follow up with a right front thrust kick to the mid section (19). (20) Step down delivering a right elbow to chin. (21) Now hit with a back knuckle, as shown. (22) Perform a Hariatoshi block. (23) Deliver a left reverse punch. Kiai point. (24) Raise left knee to left elbow readying for attack. (25) Step down into natural stance doing a left Shuto to the throat area. (26) Move left leg back in a 45° angle readying for Mawashi Uke block. (27) Perform Mawashi Uke block.

Gekisai

The man shifts his back leg to oppose to his opponent who is just reaching for him. Man shifts his back arm in front of the chest. Pics. (17 - 19) (see Man or Kata). Look at pic. (20) and pic. (21) while he pulls out his right hand in front of the chest and at the same time he extends his back arm against the incoming hand. Let his block this reverse flow which is shown in pic. (22). Pics. (23) (see Man or Kata in pic. 10).

Gekisai Ni

(28) Move right leg back in the opposite direction (45° angle) readying for Mawashi Uke block. Perform Mawashi Uke block (29). (30) Step down with left foot while moving right foot straight ahead into cat stance position once more readying for Mawashi Uke block. (31) Perform Mawashi Uke block. (32) Bring right foot back, ending kata. Kata finished (33).

SANCHIN
⟨3 battles⟩

Interpreted as the 3 battles or move 3 steps forward. This is one of the two basic katas of the Goju system. This kata represents the HARD (GO) kata. It uses only sanchin-dachi and simple, basic, hand movements stressing coordination. In a philosophical way it is the most difficult of all katas to perfect, because of the entire use of fundamentals only. There are no techniques per se. It emphasizes self-training, breathing, and mind-control. There is an emphasis on power training isometric concentration of all the muscles that are involved in fighting and self-defense.

Sanchin

(1) Mucso position. (2) On guard ready position. Right foot comes forward into Sanchin stance (3). (All stances in this kata are Sanchin Dachi). Both hands come up into 2 Chudan Uke blocks. (4) Left hand comes back into chamber. (5) Left hand punches out, aiming for opponent's solar plexus. Left hand comes to elbow from the punch (6). (7) Block is completed with left hand. (8) Stepping forward with the left foot while hand comes to chamber. (9) Right hand aims punch at solar plexus.

11

14

Sanchin

(10) Right hand does middle area block, passing left elbow (see photo 6). (11) Right foot steps forward, left hand comes to chamber. (12) Left hand punches right elbow. (13) Right leg comes up in air. Right foot stomps down doing Fumikomi stomping kick (14). Untwist, moving to the back readying left arm to do middle block (15). (16) Do middle block. (17) Do right solar plexus punch. (18) Turn the punch into a middle block.

17

18

Sanchin

Step forward with right foot, (19) retract left arm to chamber. (20) Punch to elbow. (21) Raise right leg in air, readying for stomp kick. (22) Do stomp kick. Untwist, doing left middle block in a left Sanchin stance (23). (24) Do right solar plexus punch. (25) Do right middle area block. (26) Step forward into right Sanchin stance. (27) Retract left arm.

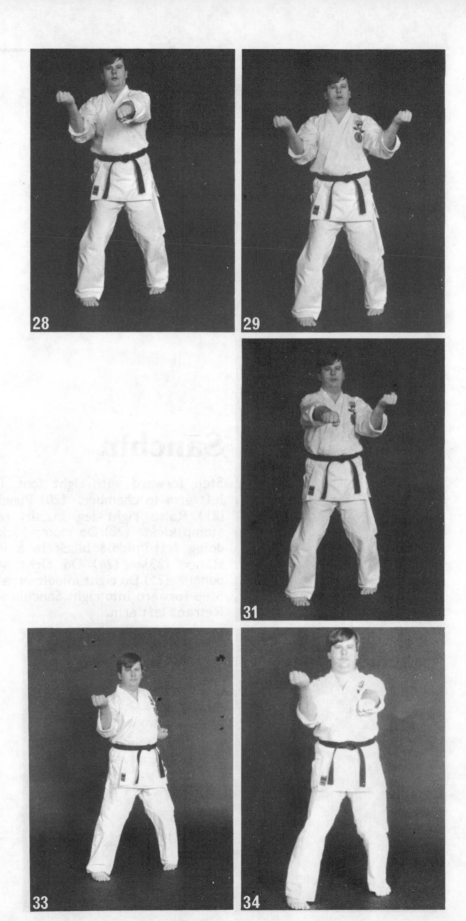

30

32

Sanchin

(28) Solar plexus punch. (29) Turn left, punch into middle block. Return right hand to chamber (30). (31) Do right solar plexus punch. (32) Turn right punch into middle block. (33) Return left arm to chamber. (34) do left punch to solar plexus. (35) Left hand retracts into middle area block. Right hand retracts into chamber (36).

35

36

Sanchin

(37) Right arm executes punch to solar plexus. Right hand moves to middle area block position (38). Both hands come together in front of chest (39). (40) Both arms push down. (41) Both arms come up crossed, shoulder height. (42) Both arms strike out simultaneously, doing Shuto.KIAI point. (43) Both arms come back chest height. (44) Both hands push down. (45) Both hands come up crossed shoulder height.

Sanchin

(46) Both hands strike out simultaneously, doing Shuto, KIAI point. Both arms come back to chest height (47). (48) Both arms push down. (49) Right foot steps back, left hand comes up to a Mawashi Uke posture. (50) Mawashi Uke block is completed. Step back with left foot readying for right Mawashi Uke (51). (52) Complete right Mawashi Uke block. (53) Step back into finished position with hands in front. (54) Kata is finished.

TENSHO
⟨turning palm⟩

Interpreted as the Turning Palm. This is the other of the two basic katas of the Goju system. This kata represents the SOFT (JU) kata. The sanchin dachi in this kata shows the outward physical power; however, the execution and movements exhibits a fighting spirit hidden below the surface. This is a blocking kata - defensive - with open hands and circular movements. The utility is in the trapping and turning opponent's power against him.

Tensho

(1) Mucso position. On guard ready position (2). (3) Step forward with right leg in Sanchin stance, execute right Uchi Uke block. (4) Open right hand. (5) Turn it over and extend right hand out in front. (6) Rotate arm off to the right and upon reaching position shown, turn hand over with palm up. (7) Draw the arm back to its original position in front with palm up. (8) Retract arm to chest area, fingers pointing up. (9) Strike out to sternum using open hand.

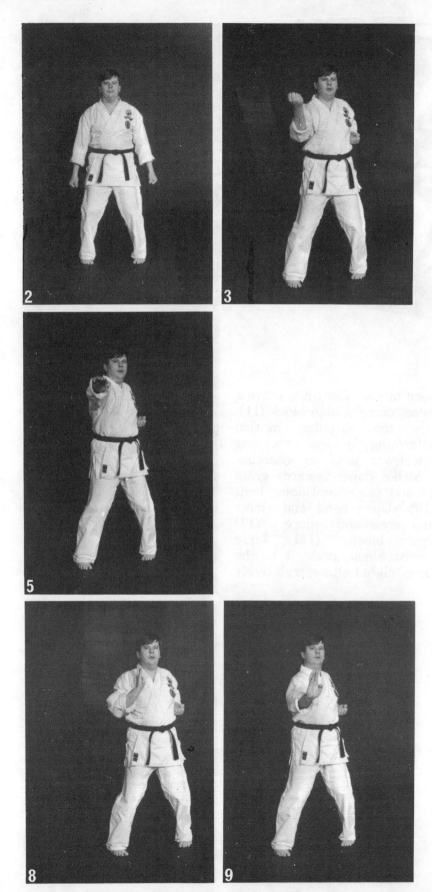

Tensho

(10) Start outward block. Continue moving right arm over head, doing a high block (11). (12) Continue the circular motion downwards, performing a low stepping block. (13) Retract arm to chamber position. (14) Strike down towards groin area. (15) Turn and raise hand doing bent wrist block. (16) Open hand and strike down on sternum area once more. (17) Perform right palm block. (18) While executing bent wrist block, draw it to the right side keeping right elbow relatively close to side.

11

12

14

17

18

Tensho

(19) Use palm heel and strike to the stomach area. (20) Step forward with left side executing left middle block. (21) Using left arm repeat steps 4 and 5. (22) Repeat step 6. (23) Repeat step 7. (24) Repeat step 8. (25) Repeat step 9. (26) Repeat step 10 and 11. (27) Repeat step 12.

Tensho

(28) Repeat step 13. (29) Repeat step 14. (30) Repeat step 15. (31) Repeat step 16. (32) Repeat step 7. (33) Repeat step 18. (34) Repeat step 19. (35) Step forward with right foot doing double middle blocks. (36) Steps 36 to 51 are as follows, (no photos). With right foot forward, using both arms repeat the sequence of steps 4 to 19 and steps 20 to 34.

Tensho

(52) Withdraw both hands to chamber. (53) Step back with right foot and push down in front. (54) Retract both hands to chamber. (55) Step back with left foot performing double palm block. (56) Step back with right foot, ready hands for Mawashi Uke block. Perform Mawashi Uke block (57). (58) Step back with left foot, ready right hand for Mawashi Uke block. (59) Perform Mawashi Uke block. (60) Bring right foot back to left, hands in front. End of kata (61).

SAIFA
⟨destroy, defeat⟩

Interpreted as Destroy, Defeat. This kata represents a proper flow from fundamental to complex techniques. It does not begin with defence only but starts off with combination techniques. Also has reverse techniques.

Saifa

(1) Mucso position. (2) On guard ready position. Right foot comes forward in Zenkutsu Dachi stance (3). Left foot comes up to right (4) with hands extended. (5) Right elbow is driven back behind you. (6) Left foot slips back in Shiko Dachi stance, arms go to your left side. (7) Left arm reaches across, blocking position. (8) Right hand strikes out, doing back hand strike. Stepping forward with left foot, (9) perform moves 3 and 4, ending with left elbow driven in behind you.

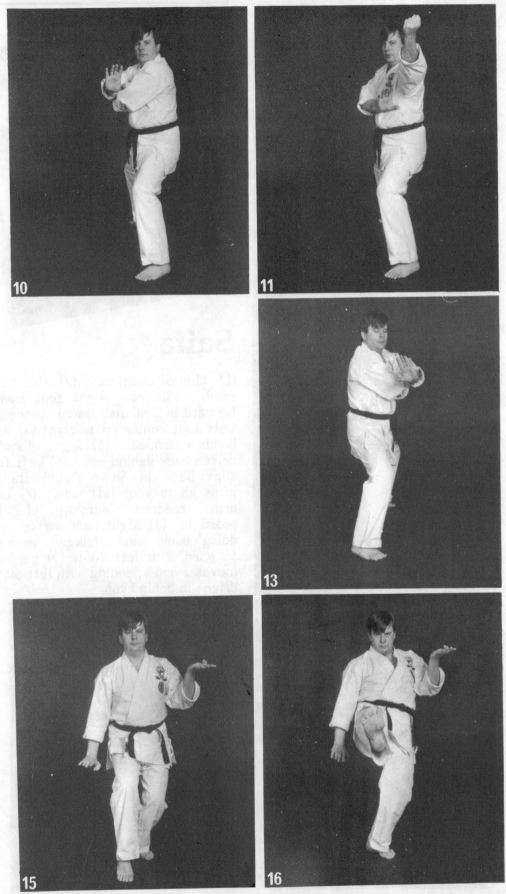

12

14

Saifa

(10) Slip right foot back into Shiko Dachi stance, blocking with the right hand. (11) Perform left back hand. (12) Stepping forward with right foot, perform moves 3 and 4 again, ending by driving right elbow in behind you. (13) Slip left foot back into Shiko Dachi, repeating number 7. (14) Repeat number 8. Move left foot 90° to your left and slide right foot over into cat stance (15). Left hand is in middle area block position, right hand in low block position, both hands are open. (16) Front kick, right foot. (17) Set down front kick in Zenkutsu Dachi stance to right, exchanging arm position. (18) Slide left foot up into cat stance position.

17

18

20

23

Saifa

(19) Perform left front kick. (20) Chamber kick. (21) Continue to step straight back, with left foot into forward stance. (22) Reach out and grab with both arms. (23) Pull both arms back in chamber. (24) Double punch. (25) Raise both hands over your head, left open, right closed. (26) Continue to circle in a downward motion, hitting with Tettsui at knee level. Move right foot up to left (27) reaching out and grabbing with both hands.

26

27

28

29

31

Saifa

33

34

30

Saifa

(28) Facing opposite direction, repeat number 23. (29) Repeat number 24. (30) Raise both arms over your head, left hand closed, right hand open. (31) Repeat number 26. (32) Raise right leg high, turn around facing front again and set down in Sanchin stance, performing right bottom fist. Immediately perform right Kake Uke (33). (34) Quickly perform Gedan Barrai with left hand. Immediately after perform right lunge punch KIAI point (35). Raise left leg, (36) turn 180° and hit with bottom fist.

32

35

36

39

Saifa

(37) Immediately perform left Kake Uke. (38) Quickly do right Gedan Barrai. Immediately deliver left lunge punch KIAI point (39). Coming up on the balls of your feet, turn clockwise ending in the position shown (40). (41) Move left foot back, then step back with right foot in cat stance, readying for half of Mawashi Uke block. Continue the Mawashi Uke block (42). (43) Strike out, completing Mawashi Uke block. (44) Step back with right foot, hands coming in front, finishing kata. (45) Kata ended.

42

45

SEIENCHIN
⟨attack, conquer & suppress⟩

Interpreted as <u>Attack, Conquer and Suppress</u> the rebellious from afar. This is the beginning of the Tiger - kata. History and tradition has animals simulated in performing the katas and the tiger was the one animal very much admired. Seienchin is therefore also known as the tiger-kata. Usually this kata is taught at the Ikkyu level, or when one is just ready for the black belt, a difficult kata to master. Until one reaches Nidan this is the main kata to practice. Sheko-dachi is emphasized and since it is the embodiment of the tiger, half of the techniques deals with attacking. There are 50 techniques in this kata and the main thrust and emphasis is on hand techniques, not leg.

Seienchin

(1) Mucso position. (2) On guard ready position. Right foot steps ahead 45° in Shiko Dachi, hands come to side (3). (4) Hands move down as shown. (5) Hands make small circle and come up head height. Both hands drop down doing low block (6). (7) Left hand crosses right, blocking punch. (8) Right hand now comes out and continues to push punch away. (9) Right hand turns over grabbing the punch.

10

13

Seienchin

Left hand strikes out in fingertip strike (10). (11) Left foot comes forward again 45°. The previous sequence is completely repeated with the left side forward covering steps, 12, 13, 14, 15, 16, 17 and 18.

16

17

Seienchin

The right foot moves forward again at a 45° angle (19) and the entire sequence is once again repeated covering steps 20, 21, 22, 23, 24, 25 and 26. The right foot steps back (27) hooking behind left, delivering right elbow at the same time. (28) Shifting forward into Sanchin stance, the left hand remains on right elbow, while the right hand swings under left, striking with a bottom fist.

Seienchin

29

Right foot steps back into Zenkutsu Dachi stance (29), left open hand does high block. (30) Left hand strikes right elbow as right foot moves up forming left Sanchin stance. KIAI point. Pivoting right at a 45° angle (31), do a right middle block augmented by left open hand. (32) Left foot steps in at 45° angle and the left hand strikes groin area. (33) Left foot steps back in a 45° angle and a full Hariatoshi block is executed, then step back. Left foot moves up facing a 45° angle (34) as the left hand does a middle block supported by right open hand. (35) Right foot steps in on a 45° angle as the right hand strikes the groin area. Right foot steps back, still at a 45° angle (36), doing a Hariatoshi block, step behind you. (37) Left foot steps back on a straight line again, simultaneously doing a head block and groin strike.

32

35

36

38

Seienchin

(38) Right foot steps back on a straight line again, step behind you. The right foot comes forward, (39) doing right Sanchin stance and a right outside Tetsue strike. (40) Right foot lifts up and hands come to chest. Step down into right Sanchin stance again doing a right upper cut KIAI point (41). Lift left foot up and do Fumikome stomp kick as hands come into position (42) readying for turn. (43) Turn to your left facing 45°, doing a left Uchi Uke block and a right Gedan Barrai block simultaneously. (44) Move right foot forward, Shiko Dachi stance, doing right half punch to the head. (45) Retract right arm doing right half punch to body. (46) Finish sequence by executing fill Hariatoshi.

41 *

44

45

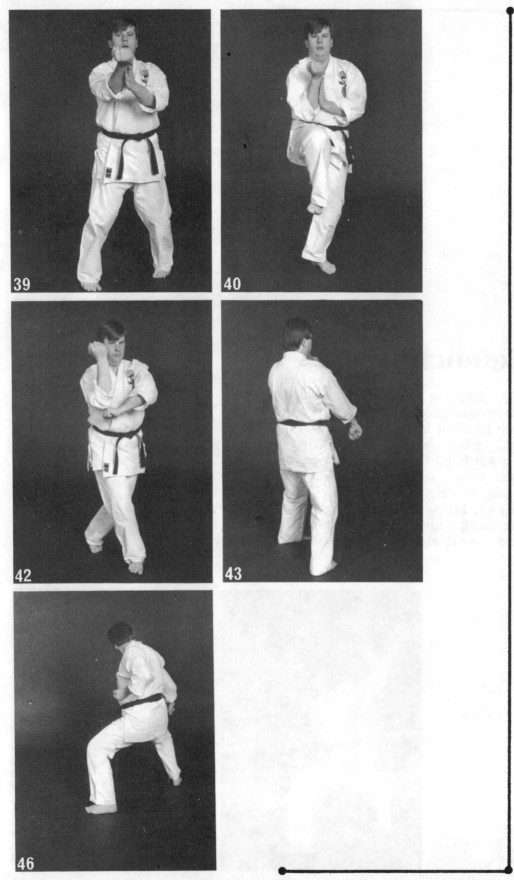

39 40 42 43 46

Seienchin

(47) Stepping behind you, do a full Hariatoshi block with your left arm. Shift right foot out into cat stance (48) delivering right elbow strike. (49) Step straight backwards into a left cat stance, delivering right elbow strike. (50) Repeat step 42, facing the right rear angle. (51) Repeat step 43, facing right rear angle. (52) Using left hand, repeat step 44. (53) Using left hand repeat step 45. (54) Using left hand repeat step 46. (55) Using right hand repeat step 47.

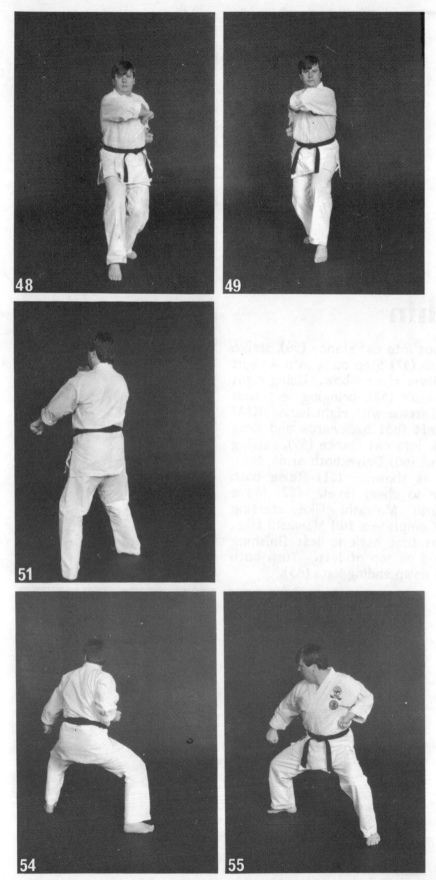

56

Seienchin

Shifting left foot into cat stance (56), strike with left elbow. (57) Step back into a right cat stance, deliver right elbow. Using right foot, jump forward (58), bringing left foot up and strike Tettsue with right hand. KIAI point. Shift left foot backwards and drag right foot back into cat stance (59), raising arms head high. (60) Drive both arms down to belt level as shown. (61) Raise both hands together to chest level. (62) Move right hand into Mawashi Uke starting position. (63) Complete a full Mawashi Uke. (64) Bring right foot back to left finishing kata, right hand on top of left. Turn both hands over and down ending kata (65).

59

62

63

SANSEIRU
⟨36 movements⟩

Interpreted as 36, some say 38. This kata philosophically emphasizes the dragon and is known as the dragon kata. It has strong attacking techniques that if applied correctly at the right time, there is no defense. It has 39 techniques with 36 of them attacking and seven kicks involved.

Sanseiru

(1) Mucso position. (2) On guard ready position. Step forward with right foot in Sanchin stance (3) both hands come up, do middle blocks. (4) Left jab. (5) Hands quickly return to position. (6) Step forward, left foot in Sanchin stance. (7) Right jab. (8) Hands quickly return to position. (9) Right forward in Sanchin stance. (10) Left jab. (11) Right hand opens and comes to left shoulder.

12

Sanseiru

(12) Right hand slides down left hand doing Shuto strike. Right foot steps back into a leaning Zenkutsu Dachi stance simultaneously doing a left palm block (13). Step straight ahead with right foot doing Zenkutsu Dachi, scooping with right hand (14), left hand readies for knee smash. (15) Right hand comes up, left hand goes down, smashing knee. Both hands do X block at groin (16). (17) Both hands are raised shoulder height, readying for elbow or wrist break. (18) Hand cross each other breaking either wrist or elbow. (19) Left Maegeri. (20) Left foot returns and steps down beside right foot. Step in with right foot, forward stance, delivering right elbow (21).

15

18

19

22

Sanseiru

(22) Left hand punches across body, right hand raises up into the air. Right elbow comes down on top of left wrist (23). Raise right leg up into position, readying for knee kick. (25) 45° knee kick. Spin around 180° facing the rear, doing a left middle block in a left Sanchin stance (26). (27) Perform right front kick. (28) Repeat step 21. (29) Punch across body with left hand. (30) Raise right arm in the air readying for elbow smash. (31) Repeat step 23.

25

28

29

32

Sanseiru

(32) Repeat step 25 and turn 90° to your left. (33) Perform left middle block. (34) Perform right front kick. (35) Repeat step 21. (36) Repeat step 29. (37) Repeat step 30. (38) Repeat step 23. (39) Repeat step 25. (40) Turn 180° to your left and perform left middle block. Perform right front kick to middle area (41).

35

38

39

Sanseiru

42

(42) Repeat step 21. (43) Punch across the body middle punch, left hand. (44) Raise right hand high, readying for elbow strike. (45) Drive elbow down on top of your own right wrist. (46) Shift left foot into Shiko Dachi and drop both hands down in front of groin area performing X block with open hands. (47) Step behind in a straight line into Shiko Dachi stance facing the front again, hands are raised high above head. Close hands and drive down finishing the throwing technique. Take note that the left hand is on top of right (48). Step right foot in front, straight ahead and perform grabbing technique, (49) right hand high, left hand low as shown. (50) Perform a foot sweep and move closed hands to designated position. (51) Step down into right Sanchin stance striking out with both hands.

45

48

49

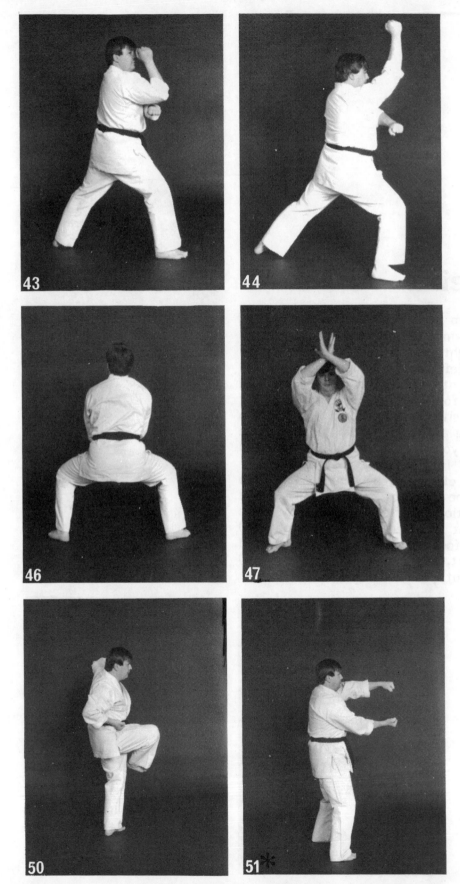

52

Sanseiru

(52) Perform right cross step. Untwist, doing a left middle block (53). (54) Step in doing a right middle block. Step ahead again with left foot in Shiko Dachi stance, (55) with right hand high and left low. (56) Raise left foot up and ready hands for punching position. Step down into Sanchin stance doing a double punch (57). (58) On the balls of your feet, spin to your right and move hands into a crane posture shoulder height with elbows slightly bent. (59) Step back with the left foot 45° in a Shiko Dachi stance positioning arms so that they cross over in what is called a dog posture. (60) Bring right foot back to left and right hand on top of left, with knees slightly bent. (61) Turn arms out, push down and finish kata.

55

58

59

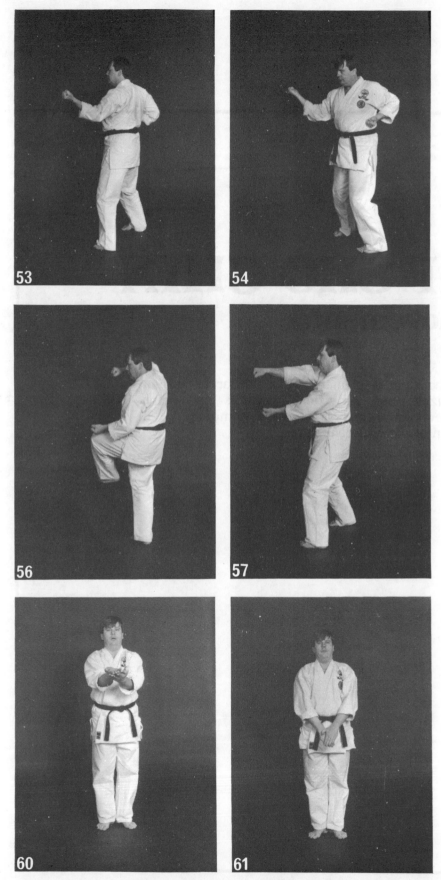

SHI SHO CHIN

⟨27 movements⟩

Shi Sho Chin is in many ways similar to Seisun. It emphasizes four directional attack and joint breaking techniques and is said by some to be a continuation of the Sanseiru Kata.

Shi Sho Chin

(1) Mucso position.   (2) On guard position. Right foot is forward in Sanchin stance (3), both hands in Uchi Uke position.   (4) Both hands fling open in Shuto position.   (5) Left hand retracts to chamber, palm up.   Left hand thrusts out to throat area (6).   (7) Left hand now turns down, fingers pointing down. (8) Left hand now retracts to the same position as step 4.   Step forward (9) with left foot in Sanchin position.

10

Shi Sho Chin

(10) Using right side repeat step 5. (11) Using right side, repeat step 6. (12) Using right side repeat step 7. (13) Using right side repeat step 8. (14) Step forward with right foot, into Sanchin stance. (15) Repeat step 5. (16) Repeat step 6. (17) Repeat step 7. (18) Repeat step 8.

13

15

16

181

Shi Sho Chin

(19) Step straight back into Zenkutsu Dachi stance bringing arms together in front of neck area. (20) Lower both arms as pictured, to belt level. (21) Step in 45° with the right foot, blocking with the right hand. (22) Left arm up to grabbing position, right hand raised for elbow break. (23) Shift the Zenkutsu Dachi stance and perform elbow break, keeping lefthand shoulder high. (24) Step forward with the left leg 45°, using left side this time. Repeat step 21. (25) Repeat steps 22 and 23. (26) Move left foot up to right, delivering right elbow to jaw. Using left forearm stepping to the left prepare for palm heel smash (27). (28) Step straight out with your left foot, turn blocking with right hand and strike to the face with the left palm.

19

22

25

26

29

Shi Sho Chin

(29) Bring left foot back to the right. (30) Stepping back with the left foot do a right palm heel strike to the face and a left palm block or groin strike. Bring left foot up to right (31). (32) Step out with left foot doing a palm heel strike. (33) Bring left foot up to right, readying for palm heel strike. (34) Step back with left foot, doing palm heel strike. (35) Step forward with your left foot in Sanchin stance, doing left Kake Uke block. (36) Perform right front thrust kick. Step down doing right elbow smash to the jaw (37). (38) Draw left foot in behind right.

32

35

36

39

Shi Sho Chin

(39) Untwist, turning 180° to your left doing a left Kake Uke block in Sanchin stance. Stepping forward do a right Kake Uke block (40). (41) Perform left front thrust kick. (42) Step forward doing left elbow strike to jaw. Bring right foot up to the left, doing a right elbow strike (43). (44) Bring left foot in behind right. (45) Untwist, doing double hand open block in cat stance. (46) Step straight into Zenkutsu Dachi stance doing double elbow strike. *(47) Other view of step 46.

42

44

45

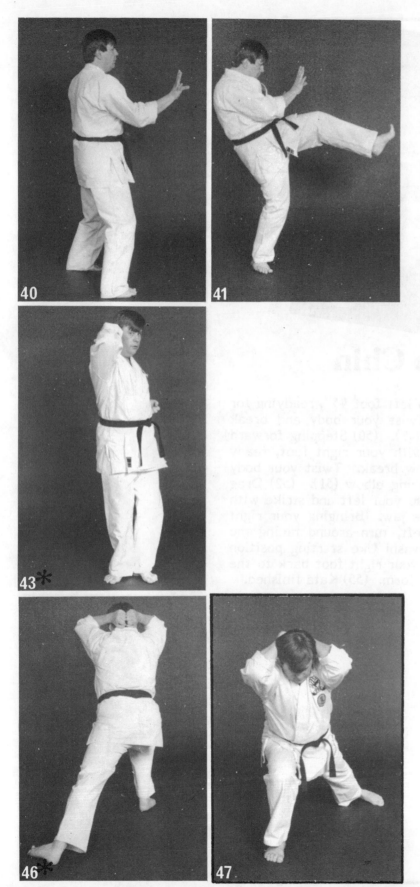

Shi Sho Guia

(49) Step in with your left foot as you execute an elbow break. Twist your body and break the boards directly. (50) Stepping forward on your right foot, face yourself for elbow break. Twist your body to the left, raising elbow. (51) Step to the right, pivot on your left and strike with the elbow to the jaw, thrusting your right fist to the left; then run around. Perform from right... Assault the set-fight position. (54)... bring your right foot back to the left, then finish...

Shi Sho Chin

(48) Step in with left foot 45°, readying for elbow break. Twist your body and break elbow as shown (49). (50) Stepping forward on a 45° angle with your right foot, ready yourself for elbow break. Twist your body to the left, breaking elbow (51). (52) Drag your right foot to your left and strike with left elbow to the jaw. Bringing your right foot in behind left, turn around facing the front into a Mawashi Uke starting position (53). (54) Bring your right foot back to the left finishing the form. (55) Kata finished.

48

51

53

SEISUN
⟨56 movements⟩

Advanced tiger kata, a continuation from Seienchin. The techniques are bolder and more advanced. From the untrained eye it looks easier than Seienchin. It involved 56 techniques with emphasis on speed and small movements. A strong emphasis on the open hand.

1

3

4

6

Seisun

(1) Mucso position (2) On guard position. Step forward with right Sanchin stance both hands doing middle block (3). (4) Left hand jabs out fast, (5) and quickly returns to block position. (6) Left foot now steps forward into Sanchin stance. Left arm jabs out. (7). (8) Right hand returns to block position.

Seisun

(9) Right foot steps forward in Sanchin position. (10) Left hand jabs out. (11) Left hand returns to middle block position. (12) Both hands fling open. (13) Right hand fingertips strike the eyes. (14) Right hand returns to position. Left hand flings out doing fingertip technique to eyes (15). (16) Return to blocking position.

Seisun

(17) Both hands fly out doing fingertip technique to eyes. (18) Right foot lifts up doing short back kick to groin, hands pull to chamber. (19) Right foot steps forward as left leg shifts forward and hands come down in front of groin area. (20) Repeat step 18. (21) Repeat step 19. (22) Repeat step 18. (23) Repeat step 19. (24) Turn 90° to your left bringing hands to chamber.

26

29

Seisun

(25) Perform low Kensetsugeri kick to knee. (26) Turn around and perform left Kake Uke, palm up. (27) Perform a small circle with left hand, grab doing a pulling Kake Uke. (28) Step forward with right foot, using right hand, repeat step 26. (29) Repeat step 27, right side. (30) Step forward, left side and repeat step 26. (31) Repeat step 27. (32) Reach out, grab throat with a reverse grip using right hand. Left hand blocks head.

31

32

33

35

36

...l kick to knee,
...der), the kne,
...all three with
... Kake-uke.
...ion, using righ
...cket shape.
...left side and
...(fig. 36-37)
...a reverse grip
...ocks 1 and.

38

39

34

37 *

Seisun

(33) Change direction, move to your right, twist and pull with your right hand. Left hand is pulled into chamber, right Sanchin stance. (34) Do a left reverse punch. (35) Do a right hand punch. Perform a right bottom fist (36). (37) Execute middle area side kick. (38) Step down with right foot, turn 180° to left and do a left palm heel first, right palm heel to groin. Step across in front into a female horse stance doing an open hand block (39). (40) Left leg steps into 45° angle in Shiko Dachi stance. (41) Perform right straight punch.

40

41

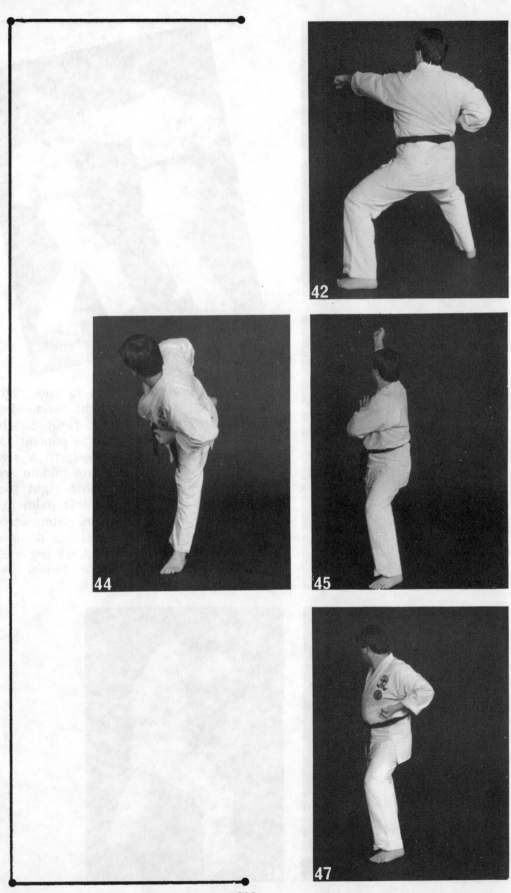

42

44

45

47

43

46

Seisun

(42) Perform left straight punch. (43) Perform right straight punch. (44) Leaving left foot where it is, perform a high side kick with left leg to the rear. (45) Step down into horse stance doing a right half punch to the face. (46) Execute right half punch to the body. Use a right Hariatoshi block (47). (48) Punch across body with left hand. (49) Use right bow and arrow punch, straight out with your right arm, to the right.

48

49

51

54

Seisun

(50) Leave hands where they are, do a right knee kick 45°. (51) Step down quickly, drop right foot behind left as arms come into Kake Uke blocking position. (52) Move left foot across to cat stance position in front, completing Kake Uke block. (53) Leave arms in front and perform strong right front kick. Step down behind and do a right down punch with left hand in front ready to block. (54). Perform a half Mawashi Uke pressing into the face and groin area (55). (56) Bring left foot back to right, finishing kata. Kata ends (57).

56

57

SEIPAI
⟨18 movements⟩

Interpreted as <u>18</u>, a continuation of the tiger form Seisun 13. It has throwing and takedown, as a tiger who pounces on his prey and finishes off as the prey is helpless on the ground.

Seipai

(1) Mucso position. (2) On guard ready position. Left foot slips straight back in Shiko Dachi, hands have begun to move (3). (4) Hands have completed the move as the right wrist has moved up and down. (5) Shift left foot up, clasp and strike middle area. Step forward, left foot, turn hands over (6). (7) Step straight back, left foot in Zenkutsu Dachi stance, bring both hands still clasped, to left shoulder. (8 & 9) In one continuous motion, move left foot straight ahead into a reverse Zenkutsu Dachi position, blocking with a left palm heel and a right high block.

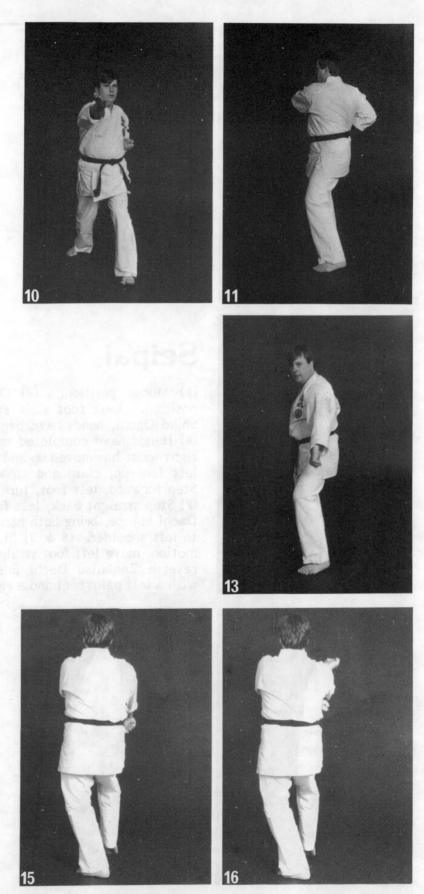

Seipai

(10) Twist straight ahead, performing a right Shuto to the neck area. (11) Move right foot to Shiko Dachi stance and punch across your body with your left hand. From there perform left back fist (12). (13) Strike straight down with a low Hariatoshi block using left hand. (14) Drag right foot to left in cat stance, do right upper cut with left hand under right elbow. From there, drop right hand down to a Gedan Barrai block (15). (16) From there, bring right hand up to middle block. (17) Open right hand and do a right Kake Uke. From there shift to female horse stance leaving hands in the same position (18).

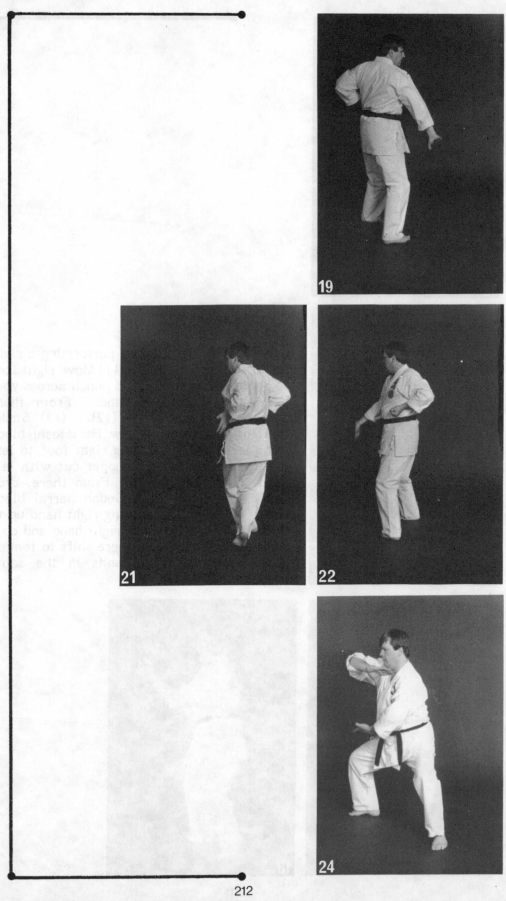

20

23

Seipai

(19) Move left foot out forming right Sanchin stance and then execute right low palm block. Step straight in and block over your head and down with your left hand (20). (21) Twist to your left and bring left hand to chamber. (22) Step forward with your right foot in Sanchin stance ($45°$) and do a right palm strike to the groin. Step in again and block as shown (23). (24) Step in deeper, bringing hands into the position shown. (25) Perform right foot sweep and ready yourself for down strike. (26) Perform double down punch.

25

26

Seipai

(27) Halfway step as shown. (28) Untwist, doing a left Hariatoshi block. Move left foot facing the opposite direction (45°) doing a palm block (29). (30) Step in front (45°) grabbing as shown. (31) Foot sweep with left foot, ready for down punch. (32) Perform double down punch. (33) Step straight back (45°), do Hariatoshi block. (34) Move left foot towards right as shown, in cat stance while blocking with both arms. Move the right leg around left and end in position shown doing arm blocking technique (35).

216

38

40

Seipai

(36) Continue the circular motion to your left, ending up in left Sanchin stance, doing left middle block. (37) Turn into low Gedan Barrai block. (38) Repeat step 36. (39) Do right middle block. (40) Do right front thrust kick. Step back into Shiko Dachi doing a left body punch (41). (42) Move left foot up to form right Sanchin stance and perform right middle block. (43) Do a low Gedan Barrai block. (44) Repeat step 42.

43

44

Seipai

(45) Add left middle block. Perform left front thrust kick (46). (47) Move back into Shiko Dachi doing right middle punch. (48) Step forward and back, with left foot forming a right cat stance with left hand low and right hand high. Step back doing cat stance and double palm block (49). (50) Raise both hands up high in blocking fashion. (51) Perform right Tetsue at belt level. (52) Move left foot back finishing kata. Kata completed (53).

Bibliography

* Kanazawa Hirokazu - Basic Karate Katas (Paul Crompton Ltd., London, England)

* Kim Richard - Classical Man (Masters Publication, Hamilton, Ontario, Canada)

* Kim Richard - Weaponless Warriors (Ohara Publication, Los Angeles, California, U.S.A.)

* Yamaguichi Gogen 'The Cat' - (Goju Kai Headquarters, Tokyo, Japan)

* Yamaguichi Gosei - Goju Ryu (Ohara Publication, Los Angeles California, U.S.A.)

* Yamaguichi Gosei - Goju Ryu Two (Ohara Publication, Los Angeles, California, U.S.A.)

* Yamamoto Gonnohyo - Karate (Tokyo, Japan)

Magazines

Black Belt: Various issues (Los Angeles, California, U.S.A.)

Karate Illustrated: Various issues (Los Angeles)

Oriental Fighting Arts: Various issues (London, England)

Also available from Masters:

The Classical Man
by
Richard Kim

Dynamic Ju Jitsu
by
Professor Wally Jay

222

About the Author

Don Warrener has been a practitioner of Goju Ryu Karate for over 15 years. He has had the good fortune to travel the world while propagating and learning the Martial Arts. The most memorable trips include Japan, England, Venezuela, Sultanate of Oman, Trinidad and France.

The author of two previous books Mr. Warrener has written several articles for international publications as well as starring in his own television series.

In 1973 and 1981 he broke a world record for breaking bricks and boards. In 1968 he won the Canadian Karate Championships while in 1973 both kata and kumite titles were his at the Eastern Canadian Championships.

Don Warrener has been taught by some of the best in the world including Benny Allen, Bob Dalgleish, Frank Lee, Dom Lopez and the legendary Gogen Yamaguichi who had a small but important part in Mr. Warrener's Martial Arts education. And of course, the one man he gives credit to for teaching him more about the Martial Arts than any other, the famous philosopher and Martial Artist Richard Kim of San Francisco.